I0817165

US Constitution

Julie Murray

Abdo Kids Junior
is an Imprint of Abdo Kids
abdobooks.com

abdobooks.com

Published by Abdo Kids, a division of ABDO, P.O. Box 398166, Minneapolis, Minnesota 55439.

Abdo Kids Junior™ is a trademark and logo of Abdo Kids.

Printed in China

052019

092019

Photo Credits: Alamy, Getty Images, iStock, National Archives and Records Administration, Shutterstock

Production Contributors: Teddy Borth, Jennie Forsberg, Grace Hansen

Design Contributors: Christina Doffing, Candice Keimig, Dorothy Toth

Library of Congress Control Number: 2018963330

Publisher's Cataloging-in-Publication Data

Names: Murray, Julie, author.

Title: US constitution / by Julie Murray.

Description: Minneapolis, Minnesota : Abdo Kids, 2020 | Series: US symbols | Includes online resources and index.

Identifiers: ISBN 9781532185397 (lib. bdg.) | ISBN 9781532186370 (ebook) | ISBN 9781532186868 (Read-to-me ebook)

Subjects: LCSH: Constitution--Juvenile literature. | Constitutions--United States--Juvenile literature. | Politics and government--Juvenile literature. | Emblems, National--United States--Juvenile literature.

Classification: DDC 342.7302--dc23

Table of Contents

US Constitution. 4

Pages of the Constitution 22

Glossary. 23

Index 24

Abdo Kids Code. 24

US Constitution

The US Constitution is a set of laws.

We the People of the United Sta
e Tranquility, provide for the common defence, promote the gener
rity, do ordain and establish this Constitution for the United State

Article. I.

All legislative Powers herein granted shall be vested in a Congress
tives.

The House of Representatives shall be composed of Members chosen
all have the Qualifications requisite for Electors of the most numerous Branch
n shall be a Representative who shall not have attained to the Age of
ot, when elected, be an Inhabitant of that State in which he shall be chosen
tatives and direct Taxes shall be apportioned among the several States wh
shall be determined by adding to the whole Number of free Persons, inclu
fifths of all other Persons. The actual Enumeration shall be made withi
y subsequent Term of ten Years, in such Manner as they shall by Law d
t, but each State shall have at Least one Representative; and until such
three, Massachusetts eight, Rhode-Island and Providence Pl
one, Maryland six, Virginia ten, North Carolina five, South Carolin

Laws are like rules. People must follow them.

STOP

It took 116 days to write.

It was signed by 39 **leaders**.

This was in 1787.

...tates, shall be bound by Oath or Affirmation, to support this Constitution; but no religious Test shall ever be ...
...lic Trust under the United States.

Article. VII.

...ventions of nine States, shall be sufficient for the Establishment of this Constitution between the Sta...

done in Convention by the Unanimous Consent of the States present the Seventeenth Day of September in the Year of our Lord one thousand seven hundred and Eighty seven an... of the Independance of the United States of America the Twelfth In witness whe... We have hereunto subscribed our Names,

...etary

Go: Washington — Presidt and deputy from Virginia

New Hampshire: John Langdon, Nicholas Gilman

Massachusetts: Nathaniel Gorham, Rufus King

Connecticut: Wm. Saml. Johnson, Roger Sherman

New York: Alexander Hamilton

New Jersey: Wil: Livingston, David Brearley, Wm. Paterson, Jona: Dayton

Pensylvania: B Franklin, Thomas Mifflin, Robt Morris, Geo. Clymer, Thos. FitzSimons, Jared Ingersoll, James Wilson, Gouv Morris

Delaware: Geo: Read, Gunning Bedford jun, John Dickinson, Richard Bassett, Jaco: Broom

Maryland: James McHenry, Dan of St Thos. Jenifer, Danl Carroll

Virginia: John Blair —, James Madison Jr.

North Carolina: Wm. Blount, Richd. Dobbs Spaight, Hu Williamson

South Carolina: J. Rutledge, Charles Cotesworth Pinckney, Charles Pinckney, Pierce Butler

Georgia: William Few, Abr Baldwin

It set up the US government.

It is made up of 3 parts.

They are called branches.

Executive

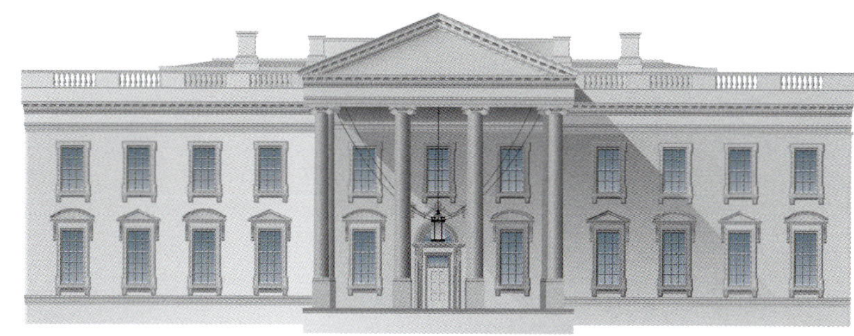

White House

Legislative

Capitol Building

Judicial

Supreme Court Building

The branches work together. They run the US. They make laws.

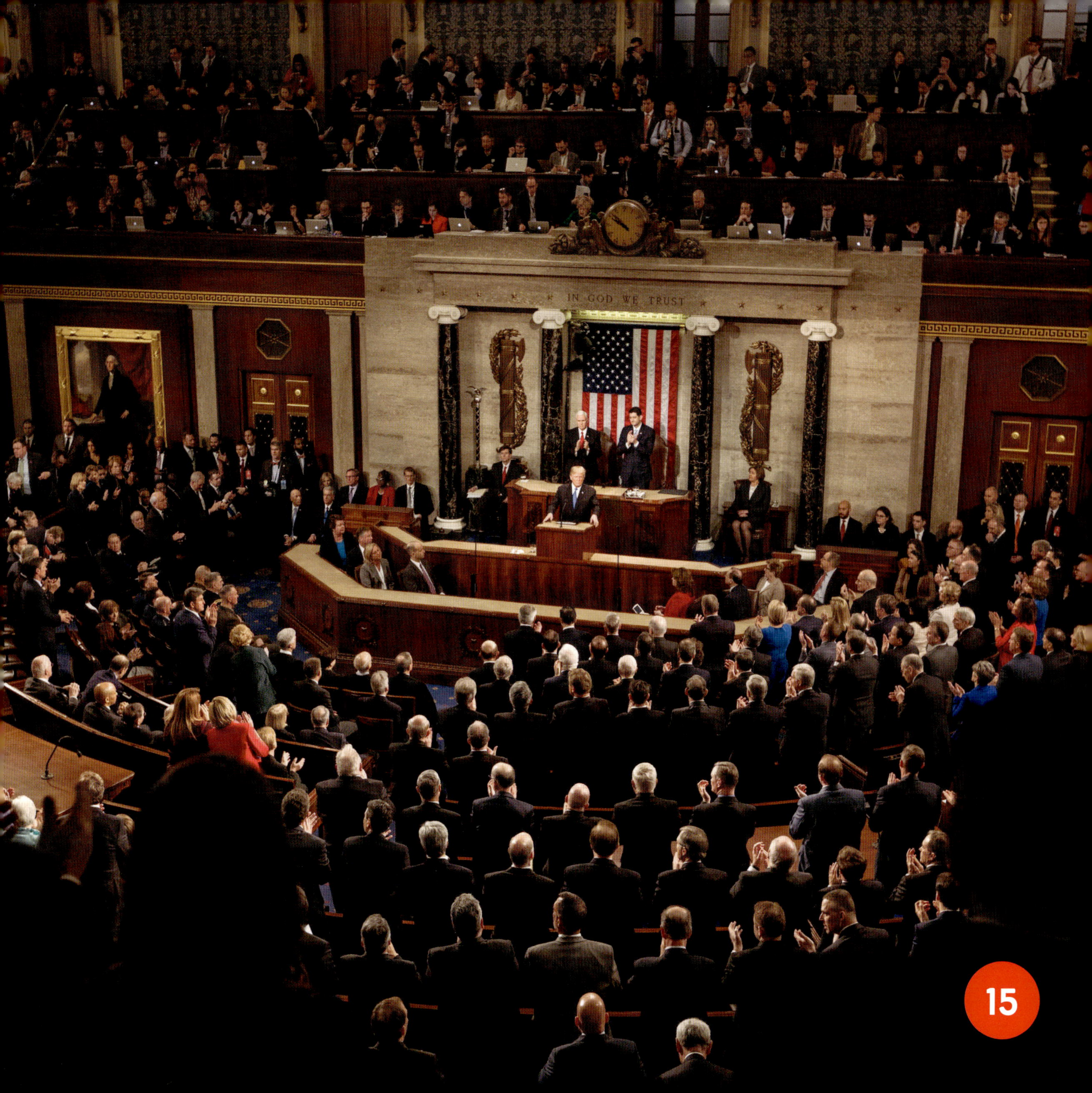
IN GOD WE TRUST

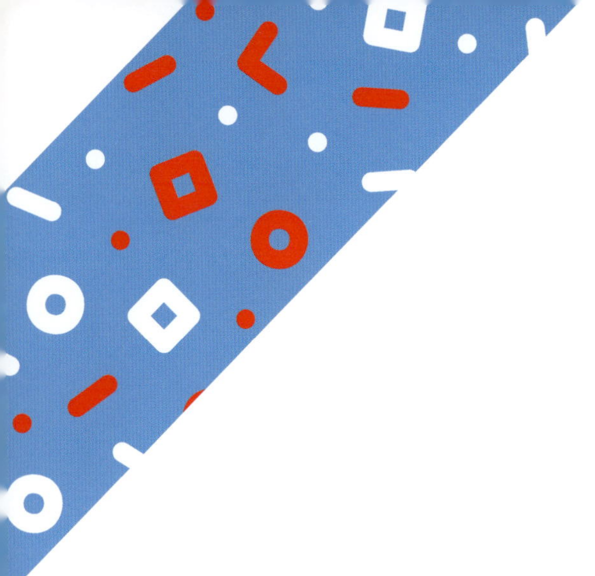

The **Bill of Rights** was added in 1791. It made 10 rule changes.

Bill of Rights

Congress of the United States,

begun and held at the City of New York, on
Wednesday, the fourth of March, one thousand seven hundred and eighty nine.

The Conventions of a number of the States having, at the time of their adopting the Constitution, expressed a desire, in order to prevent misconstruction or abuse of its powers, that further declaratory and restrictive clauses should be added: And as extending the ground of public confidence in the Government, will best insure the beneficent ends of its institution:

Resolved, by the SENATE and HOUSE of REPRESENTATIVES of the UNITED STATES of AMERICA in Congress assembled, two thirds of both Houses concurring. That the following Articles be proposed to the Legislatures of the several States, as Amendments to the Constitution of the United States; all, or any of which articles, when ratified by three fourths of the said Legislatures, to be valid to all intents and purposes, as part of the said Constitution, viz.

Articles in addition to, and Amendment of the Constitution of the United States of America, proposed by Congress, and ratified by the Legislatures of the several States, pursuant to the fifth Article of the Original Constitution.

Article the first ...... After the first enumeration required by the first Article of the Constitution, there shall be one Representative for every thirty thousand, until the number shall amount to one hundred, after which, the proportion shall be so regulated by Congress, that there shall be not less than one hundred Representatives, nor less than one Representative for every forty thousand persons, until the number of Representatives shall amount to two hundred, after which, the proportion shall be so regulated by Congress, that there shall not be less than two hundred Representatives, nor more than one Representative for every fifty thousand persons. [Not Ratified]

Article the second .... No law, varying the compensation for the services of the Senators and Representatives, shall take effect, until an election of Representatives shall have intervened. [Not Ratified]

Article the third .... Congress shall make no law respecting an establishment of religion, or prohibiting the free exercise thereof; or abridging the freedom of speech, or of the press; or the right of the people peaceably to assemble, and to petition the Government for a redress of grievances.

Article the fourth ..... A well regulated Militia, being necessary to the security of a free State, the right of the people to keep and bear Arms, shall not be infringed.

Article the fifth .... No Soldier shall, in time of peace, be quartered in any house, without the consent of the owner, nor in time of war, but in a manner to be prescribed by law.

Article the sixth ...... The right of the people to be secure in their persons, houses, papers, and effects, against unreasonable searches and seizures, shall not be violated, and no Warrants shall issue but upon probable cause, supported by oath or affirmation, and particularly describing the place to be searched, and the persons or things to be seized.

Article the seventh ... No person shall be held to answer for a capital, or otherwise infamous crime, unless on a presentment or indictment of a grand jury, except in cases arising in the land or Naval forces, or in the Militia, when in actual service in time of War or public danger; nor shall any person be subject for the same offence to be twice put in jeopardy of life or limb; nor shall be compelled in any criminal case, to be a witness against himself, nor be deprived of life, liberty, or property, without due process of law; nor shall private property be taken for public use without just compensation.

Article the eighth ..... In all criminal prosecutions, the accused shall enjoy the right to a speedy and public trial by an impartial jury of the State and district wherein the crime shall have been committed, which district shall have been previously ascertained by law, and to be informed of the nature and cause of the accusation; to be confronted with the witnesses against him; to have compulsory process for obtaining witnesses in his favor, and to have the assistance of counsel for his defence.

Article the ninth ...... In suits at common law, where the value in controversy shall exceed twenty dollars, the right of trial by jury shall be preserved, and no fact, tried by a jury, shall be otherwise re-examined in any Court of the United States, than according to the rules of the common law.

Article the tenth ...... Excessive bail shall not be required, nor excessive fines imposed, nor cruel and unusual punishments inflicted.

Article the eleventh .. The enumeration in the Constitution, of certain rights, shall not be construed to deny or disparage others retained by the people.

Article the twelfth .... The powers not delegated to the United States by the Constitution, nor prohibited by it to the States, are reserved to the States respectively, or to the people.

Frederick Augustus Muhlenberg Speaker of the House of Representatives.

ATTEST,

John Adams, Vice President of the United States, and President of the Senate.

John Beckley, Clerk of the House of Representatives.

Sam. A. Otis Secretary of the Senate.

More changes were made. One gave women the right to vote.

VOTE
VOTE
VOTE
VOTE
VOTE

It is in a **museum**. You can see it today!

CONSTITUTION
OF THE
UNITED STATES OF AMERICA

Pages of the Constitution

It begins, "We, the people of the United States..."

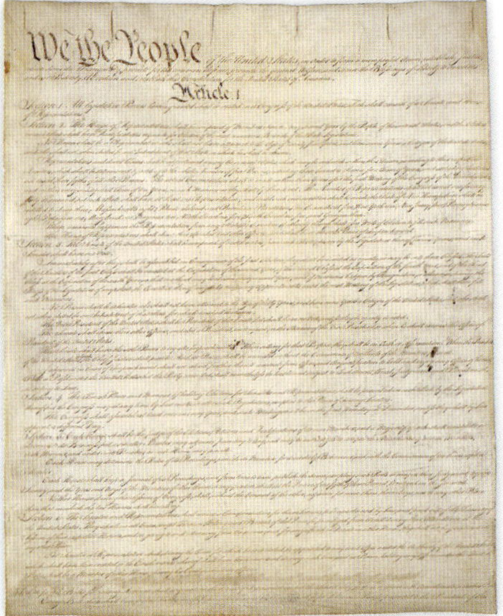
We the People
Article I

Article III
Article IV

Article II

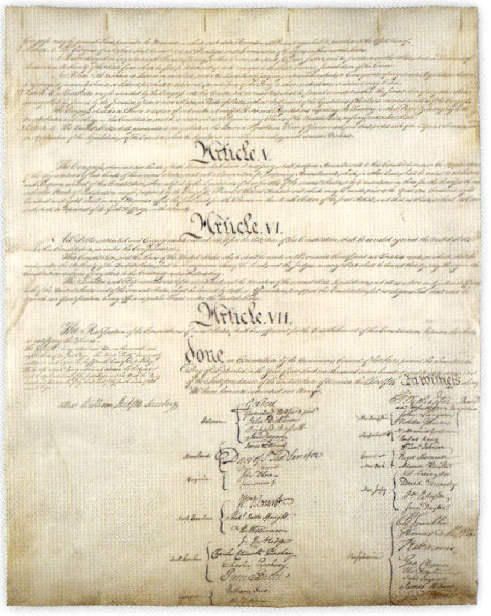
Article V
Article VI
Article VII
Done

signatures

Glossary

Bill of Rights
rules added to the constitution that gave people certain freedoms and gave clear limits to the government.

leaders
people who help guide others. George Washington was a leader who helped write the US Constitution.

museum
a building where objects that are important to history, art, or science are kept and shown to the public.

Index

Bill of Rights 16

branches 12, 14

creation 8

government 12

laws 4, 6, 14

leaders 10

museum 20

signatures 10

vote 18

women's rights 18

Visit **abdokids.com** to access crafts, games, videos, and more!

Use Abdo Kids code

UUK5397

or scan this QR code!